Research in Wireless Sensor Networks

S.Kannadhasan

M.Shanmuganantham

Dr. R.Nagarajan

C.Gurunathan

ELIVA PRESS

S.Kannadhasan

M.Shanmuganantham

Dr. R.Nagarajan

C.Gurunathan

Remote Sensor Networks (WSNs) have a developing innovation for different applications in reconnaissance, condition, natural surroundings observing, medicinal services and fiasco administration. It has monitor through environment by using sensing device that means of physical properties. WSN is a network that can transmit and receive through the wireless medium by using the sensor devices for various nodes. There are various base stations to control final destination of data from one place to other place. It includes the dense ad-hoc deployment, dynamic topology, spatial distribution, and Network topology, Graph Theory with constraint the bandwidth, energy life time and memory. Based on the problem size increases, it can require as various efforts by using the optimization techniques. This paper is to distinguish the deficiencies in Wireless Sensor Networks the hubs have transmitted starting with one place then onto the next by utilizing the particle swarm enhancement. PSO calculation is contrasted and the different calculations PCA, Neural system and OPAST. Based on the algorithm, the performance analysis is done on specificity, fault detection and fault coverage. The simulation result shows the energy life time, throughput, packet delivery ratio produces good performance when compared to the other algorithms.

Published: Eliva Press SRL
Address: MD-2060, bd.Cuza-Voda, 1/4, of. 21 Chişinău, Republica
Moldova
Email: info@elivapress.com
Website: www.elivapress.com

ISBN: 978-1-952751-15-8

Research in Wireless Sensor Networks

S. Kannadhasan

B.E.,M.E.,M.B.A.,PGDCA.,PGVLSI.,PGDRD.,MISTE.,MIE.,MIETE.,PGEMD.,
M.A.,M.Sc.,PGDBI.,(Ph.D)

Assistant Professor

Department of Electronics and Communication Engineering

Cheran College of Engineering

Karur, Tamilnadu-639111

M. Shanmuganantham

B.E., M.I.S.T.E

Lecturer (S.G) and Vice Principal

Department of Electrical and Electronics Engineering

Engineering Tamilnadu Polytechnic College Madurai-625011

Dr.R.Nagarajan

B.E., M.E., Ph.D

Professor

Gnanamani College of Technology

Namakkal-637018

C.Gurunathan

B.E., M.E

Lecturer

Department of Electrical and Electronics Engineering

Engineering Tamilnadu Polytechnic College Madurai-625011

TABLE OF CONTENT

Chapter 1 – Particle Swarm Optimization Algorithm

1.1 Overview

Remote Sensor Networks (WSNs) have a developing innovation for different applications in reconnaissance, condition, natural surroundings observing, medicinal services and fiasco administration. It has monitor through environment by using sensing device that means of physical properties. WSN is a network that can transmit and receive through the wireless medium by using the sensor devices for various nodes. There are various base stations to control final destination of data from one place to other place. It includes the dense ad-hoc deployment, dynamic topology, spatial distribution, and Network topology, Graph Theory with constraint the bandwidth, energy life time and memory. Based on the problem size increases, it can require as various efforts by using the optimization techniques. This paper is to distinguish the deficiencies in Wireless Sensor Networks the hubs have transmitted starting with one place then onto the next by utilizing the particle swarm enhancement. PSO calculation is contrasted and the different calculations PCA, Neural system and OPAST. Based on the algorithm, the performance analysis is done on specificity, fault detection and fault coverage. The simulation result shows the energy life time, throughput, packet delivery ratio produces good performance when compared to the other algorithms.

1.2 Introduction

WSNs have comprise consists of sensors which are classified for collecting, information, processing, storing and transferring information from one node to another in a wireless manner [1]-[5]. These WSN sensors the nodes work with physical phenomenon have some intelligence through network; each other to sense some data can be processed the sensors through the network. Wireless sensor networks consist of protocols and algorithms with increases the life time of sensor networks. Wireless sensor networks mainly used for temperature, pressure, humidity, noise levels, lighting conditions which is used for broadcast communication that means of point-to-point communication[6]-[10]. Wireless sensor networks have limited by power, energy and network capability.

The WSN applications are classified in three categories:

- Devices Monitoring.
- Network area Monitoring.
- Both Network area and Devices Monitoring.

WSN can be used for low power wireless communication for sensors. WSN are often deployed in inaccessible and inhospitable environments throughout the world. Principal component analysis (PCA) is the most popular methods for data transmitted for wide range of applications [11]-[13]. The various numerical techniques are used to calculate the numerical techniques or cross correlation relationship between the variables in the data variables by using the algorithm [14]-[15]. Zone-based routing (like OPAST) is an algorithm, that divided the small number of networks zone which is the area covered by the sensor networks.

1.3 Structure of the Algorithm

In this paper, based on the algorithm they address the problem of outlier detection in WSNs. They provide a technique-based algorithm framework to detect the techniques designed for WSNs. The proposed algorithm introduces the node characteristic and description of different detection techniques .Based on the detection techniques to compare the various sensor nodes for detection. This paper proposes a monitoring and diagnosis with dynamic power for applying the WSNs devices for various signal acquisition, processing, and transmission. The Proposed algorithm, the nodes which are responsible received the data collection and transmitting through supervisory controller. DPM protocol is used for sensor nodes to increases the Wireless Sensor Network lifetime; this proposed work presents past and present conditions of the PSO algorithm.

If the nodes are failed for fault detection algorithm, by using particle Swarm Optimization (PSO) is efficient in fault detection when the nodes are enormous. Each node is to be consider the particle and travelling with velocity with function of optimized P_{best} (personal best) value with V (t). P_{best} and Gbest value is used to optimize techniques for the network to detect the faulty node. PSO algorithm is used to easy the detect the fault nodes that compare other techniques.

Advantages of PSO over other conventional algorithms are:

1) Easy way to implement the hardware or software.
2) Based on the parameters to check availability of the network.
3) Real, integer and binary domains are also check the parameters using this algorithm.

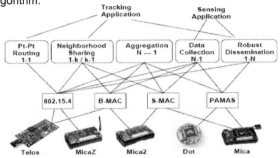

Figure.1. Architecture of WSN

1.4 Module of the Proposed Method

In PSO method, is used to calculate each potential node solution and every solution has positions $(T_{i,j})$ and $(S_{i,j})$. The solution set of the each solution that means of swarm. Based on the algorithm, each solution is used to generate random numbers from the solution space in the WSN network. Based on the algorithm, the solution of each solution and the swarm is kept as Far best $(F_{besti,j})$ and Whole best $(H_{besti,j})$, respectively. Based on the method, the calculation of solution and position of each node is shown in below (1) and (2).

$$X_{i,j}(t+1)=ME_{i,j}(t) + D_lQ_1(F_{besti,j} - T_{i,j}(t)) + D_2Q_2(H_{besti,j} - T_{i,j}(t)) \tag{1}$$

$$T_{i,j}(t+1) = T_{i,j}(t) + X_{i,j}(t+1) \tag{2}$$

Where i and j is the index of the solution and position network. T shows the iteration number, $X_{i,j}(t)$ is the solution of the ith and j^{th} indexof the particle in the swarm and $T_{i,j}(t)$ is the position. Q_1 and Q_2 are used to generate the random numbers uniformly distributed between the range of 0 and 1 .D_1 and D_2 are the acceleration numbers. M is the inertial weight. The implementing PSO algorithm for each solution is given below:

1. Each solution has generated random number with suitable dimensional feature.
2. Each particle has calculated by using the formula.
3. The success of the current solution is better than the success of $F_{besti,j}$ then determine $F_{besti,j}$ as the current solution.
4. Current particle is used to determine the success of $G_{besti,j}$ is better than the current solution.
5. Calculate the solution and position of the particle using (1) and (2).
6. Follow the steps from 2 to 5 maximum iteration is reached.

Inertial weight is, $M = t_{max} - t/t_{max}$

Where M is inertial weight, t and t_{max} corresponds to the current iteration number and maximum iteration number. The parameters D_1 and D_2 are used to determine the particle in terms of local or global solutions in solution space. PSO method is used to identify the iteration that means of constant D_1 and D_2 are both equal to 2 for all applications.

1.5 Particle Swarm Optimization Algorithm

PSO Explanation

Y is the representation of T in the new basis:

Y= PT

R is the covariance matrix in the new basis:

$$R_y = \frac{1}{n-1} Y Y_T \tag{3}$$

Covariance matrix is defined as

- Matrix Defined:
  S= TT'
- S is symmetric.
- Symmetric matrix is used to calculate by an orthogonal matrix of its eigenvectors.

$$Ry = \frac{1}{n-1} YY_T = \frac{1}{n-1}(PT)(PXT) = \frac{1}{n-1} PXTPXT \tag{4}$$

Subspace methods have calculated in solving various statistical problems in array signal processing channel estimation and code-division multiple access (CDMA) communications. Based on EVD, subspace methods on same matrices using space decomposition.

1.6 Simulation Results And Discussion

PSO algorithm is used to detect the energy efficiency of best node for the process data transmitted through the network. The proposed techniques, numbers of valid packets are dropped when the rate is increased in the malicious nodes shows the increase in throughput of the network. The numbers of packets are received when the data is transmitted to the sink successfully. The Proposed techniques are increased in throughput of the network.

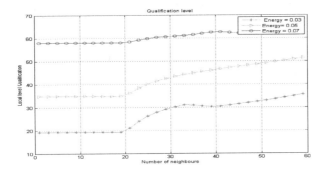

Figure.2 Analysis of Neighbour Node

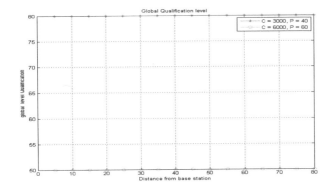

Figure. 3. Analysis of Distance of Various Nodes

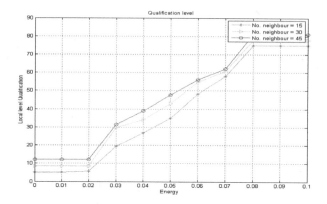

Figure. 4. Analysis of Distance of Various Nodes based PSO

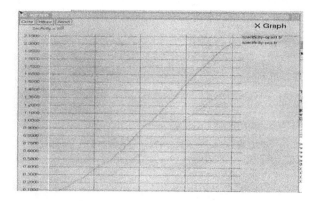

Figure.5.Packet Delivery Ratio

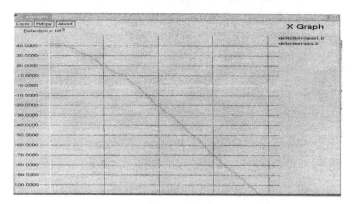

Figure.6. Average Energy Consumption

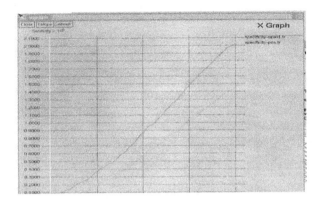

Figure.7. Throughput of the Network

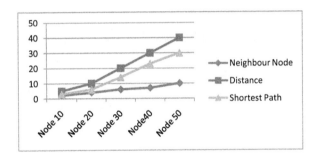

Figure.8. Comparison of Various Nodes

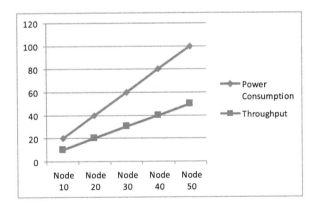

Figure.9. Power Consumption of various Nodes

7

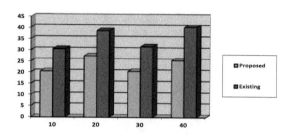

Figure.10. Power Consumption of the Proposed and Existing Network

1.7 Conclusion and Future Scope

PSO algorithm has been a popular technique is used to solve optimization problems in WSNs due to its easy, quality, fast coverage and insignificant computational burden. The simulation result shows that PSO produces good performance when compared to the other conventional algorithms. WSN network has challenge of reduced life time through network with the support like energy consumption of nodes is higher. The proposed method is used to analyse the various parameters like distance, power consumed and trust value by using PSO technique classifies the given sensor nodes into F and H Best Node. Future research on PSO method in WSN applications like: 1) Real world applications. 2) Development of PSO in hardware. 3) Development of parameters based on the network.

References

1. Tian, D., Georganas, M.D.: " A coverage-preserving node scheduling scheme for large wireless sensor networks ". WSNA'02: Proc. First ACM Int. Workshop on Wireless Sensor Networks and Applications, 2002, pp. 32-41.

2. Cardei, M., Thai, M.T., Yingshu, L., Weili, W.: " Energy-efficient target coverage in wireless sensor networks ". INFOCOM 2005: 24th Annual Joint Conf. IEEE Computer and communications Societies, 2005, pp. 1976-1984.

3. Huang, D.-F., Tseng, Y.-C.: " The coverage problem in a wireless sensor network ". WSNA'03: Proc. Second ACM Int. Conf. on Wireless Sensor Networks and Applications, 2003, pp. 115-121.

4. Chih-fan, H., Mingyan, L.: " Network coverage using low duty-cycled sensors: random & coordinated sleep algorithms ". IPSN'04: Proc. Third Int. Symp. On Information Processing in Sensor Networks, 2004, pp. 433-442.

5. Zhang, H., Wang, H., Feng, H.: " A distributed optimum algorithm for target coverage in wireless sensor networks". Asia-Pacific Conf. on Information Processing, 2009, pp. 144-147.

6. Fuad Bajaber, Irfan Awan.: Adaptive decentralized re-clustering protocol for wireless sensor networks, Journal of computer and Systems sciences, doi:10.1016/j.jcss.2010.01.007.

7. Yi-hua zhu, Wan-deng wu, Jian pan, Yi-ping tang.: An energy efficient data gathering algorithm to prolong lifetime of wireless sensor networks, Computer Communications 33, pp. 639-647 (2010).

8. Fuad Bajaber, Irfan Awan.: Energy efficient clustering protocol to enhance lifetime of wireless sensor network, Journal of Ambient Intelligence and Human Computing 1, pp. 239-248 (2010).

9. N.Dimokas, D.Katsaros,Y.Manolopoulos.: Energy-efficient distributed clustering in wireless sensor networks, Journal of Parallel and Distributed Computing 70, pp. 371-383 (2010).

10. Jamal N. Al-Karaki, Raza Ul-Mustafa, Ahmed E. Kamal, "Data Aggregation in Wireless Sensor Networks - Exact and Approximate Algorithms'", Proceedings of IEEE Workshop on HighPerformance Switching and Routing (HPSR), USA.

11. Suman Banerjee, Archan Misra, "Adapting Transmission Power for Optimal Energy Reliable Multi-hop Wireless Communication", Wireless Optimization Workshop (WiOpt'03), Sophia-Antipolis, France, March 2003.

12. Niranjan Kumar Ray, Ashok Kumar Turuk, "Energy Efficient Techniques for Wireless Ad Hoc Network",

13. Shan Lin, Jingbin Zhang, Gang Zhou, Lin Gu, Tian He, and John A. Stankovic,"ATPC: Adaptive Transmission Power Control for Wireless Sensor Networks", SenSys '06 Proceedings of the 4th international conference on Embedded networked sensor systems, Pages 223-236

14. S.G.Shirinivas, S.Vetrivel, N.M.Elango "Applications of Graph Theory in Computer Science - An Overview", International Journal of Engineering Science and Technology, Vol. 2(9), 2010, 4610-4621

15. Bhupendra Gupta , Srikanth K Iyer , D Manjunath , "Topological Properties Of The One Dimensional Exponential Random Geometric Graph", Random Structures & Algorithms , Volume 32 , Issue 2 , 2008, pp: 181-204 [18] Chen Avin , "Random Geometric Graphs: An Algorithmic Perspective" , Ph,D dissertation, University of California , Los Angeles , 2006

Chapter 2- Transmission Power Using Shortest Path

2.1 Overview

Energy efficiency in wireless sensor network [WSN] is the highly important role for the researchers. This transmission power technique come under two broad categories called tree based approach and clustering techniques. In these techniques clustering is the important factors for real time applications. This paper presents the importance of the sensor nodes and factors affecting the clustering. The proposed the clustering technique using Minimum Spanning Tree [MST] and shortest path concept with its strength and limitations. The Comparison of Clustering technique based distance between from the Local Level and Neighbour Node transmission in wireless sensor networks.

2.2 Introduction

Wireless sensor networks (WSNs) have become a hot research topic in recent years clustering is considered as an effective approach to reduce network overhead and improve scalability. Wireless sensor network is one of the pervasive networks which sense our environment through various parameters like heat, temperature, pressure, etc...[1]Since sensor networks are based on the dense deployment of disposable and low-cost sensor nodes, destruction of some nodes by hostile action does not affect a military operation as much as the destruction of a traditional sensor, which makes the sensor network concept a better approach for battlefields. [2]. The transmission between the two nodes will minimize the other nodes to show the improve throughput and greater than spatial reuse than wireless networks to lack the power controls. Adaptive Transmission Power technique to improve the Network Life Time in Wireless Sensor Networks using graph theory [3].We have distance comparison between the neighbour nodes and also local level connected from the nearest edges in wireless sensor networks.

2.3 Related Work

Once the clustering procedure , each node in the network is associated with a cluster head. Two clusters in a neighbour node have high enough contact probability (≥γ), a pair of gateway nodes are identified to bridge them. Consider Node i, which intends to send a data message to Node j. Node i looks up its cluster table to find the cluster ID of Node j, i.e., Ω_j [4] . According to Ω_j , three types are considered: intra and inter cluster routing, one-hop and also multihop inter-cluster routing.

2.4 Proposed Work

The Clustering Technique using the minimum spanning tree[MST] to detect the shortest path in wireless sensor networks. The data from near by the cluster heads will be directly transmitted to the sink node. The data from sink nodes to calculate the distance whereas the cluster head will be transmitted through the shortest multihop path [5].The distance between the cluster head and sink node. The shortest path between each cluster head to the sink node. To find the Predominant node[Maximum number of path].Transmission power techniques is to improve the performance of the network in several aspects. Transmission range in the wireless networks should be change the ranges in each link. The traffic capacity decreases when more nodes are added to increases the interference[6].Routing graph theory to multiple paths from data sources to a neighbours node. A Novel approach Adaptive state based clustering, which demonstrate the directed acyclic graphs from each node to gateways between any given cluster head[7]. We have the local level distance from the edge from the nearest connected to the neighbouring nodes[8]. We have two approaches the transmission power to improve the network life time in wireless sensor networks.

• Tree based approach

• Clustering based approach

2.5 Clustering approach

In the cluster-based approach sensor nodes in particular WSN are permitted to transmit sensed data towards the base station. In this allows sensor nodes to sense and transmit the sensed information to the cluster-heads directly, instead of routing through its immediate neighbors. When a cluster node fails because of energy depletion we need to choose alternative cluster for that particular region. In periodical time each sensor node in the cluster should possess the next cluster head re-election based on energy to avoid node failure. Unlike previous algorithms, cluster formation precedes before cluster head selection. This is Graph Theory based on Minimum Spanning Tree (MST) concept. The spanning tree is 'minimal' to the cluster of each node when the total length of the edges is the minimum necessary to connect all the vertices in the clustering head. But in our proposed algorithm MST is used in the initial source node formation phase and each cluster head formation phase[Figure 1]..

2.6 Cluster Head Selection

In the newly formed clusters, the each node with the highest energy level is selected as the cluster head and the next higher energy level node is selected as the next CH node.

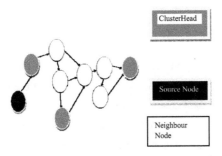

ClusterHead

Source Node

Neighbour
Node

Figure 1 : Network Structure

2.7 Algorithm

1. Start the Program

2. Read the Number of Nodes and Cluster head

3. Read the Number of Edges

4. Read the Number of Neighbour Nodes

5. Label the Start edges as 0.

6. Label of each edges is connected to the edges with its distance.

7. From this edges, consider the distance to each connected edges.

8. If the edges is greater than one of its edges, to calculate the distance and also read the distance

9. If the edges is less than one of its edges to calculate the distance and also read the distance.

10. If there is no distance at the edges, write down the new distance.

11. Calculate the Shortest path Detection.

12. Read the Local Level distance.

2.8 Transmission Power Using Shortesh Path

Networks can be represented by clustering approach. The distance between two vertices of cluster head node i and j is the length of a shortest path joining them and is denoted by D[i,j]. If there is no path between cluster head of each node joining i and j then we define as D[i,j]=0. First we initialize the transmission power is denoted R. If the node i is less than number of edges are connected to the each cluster head node selection then get the distance between the edges to transmitted power in the networks. Final we calculate the Total power consumed of the whole networks.

2.9 Results and Discussion

The performance of our Transmission power technique is through MATLAB. Cluster Head selection using the main parameters like shortest path and power consumed using the transmission power technique [Figure 2]. Figure 3 shows that the performance of Neighbour Node Identification. Figure 4 shows that the performance of the distance calculation of the networks. Figure 5 shows that the performance of the distance based local level calculation of the networks

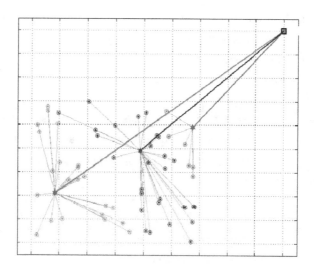

Figure 2: Cluster Head Selection

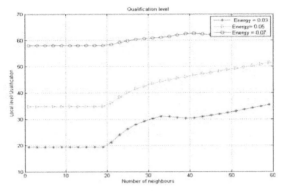

Figure 3: Neighbour Node

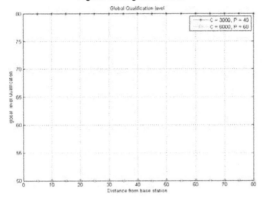

Figure 4: Distance Calculation

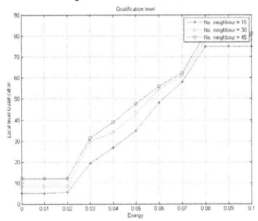

Figure 5: Distance based Local Level Qualification

2.10 Conclusion

The proposed system of clustering approach using Transmission power technique is based on Graph theory to enhance the lifetime of the entire sensor network. The eligible sensor nodes are chosen depending on their power levels and association with number of nodes in transmission area. The efficiency of the proposed model is experimented and evaluated in Matlab and the results accomplished showed that in this technique, sensor nodes utilize extremely less power and stay in the network for a greater period of time.

References

[1] Akyildiz F., "A Survey on Sensor Networks," Computer Journal of IEEE Communications Magazine, vol. 40, no. 8, pp. 102-114, 2002.

[2] Yingshu Li, My T. Thai, Weili Wu, Wireless sensor networks and applications, Springer, 2008 - Computers - 441 pages

[3] Zou, Y. Chakrabarty, K. , Energy-aware target localization in wireless sensor networks, Pervasive Computing and Communications, Proceedings of the First IEEE International Conference on 2003. (PerCom 2003)

[4] Amit Sharma, Kshitij Shinghal, Neelam Srivastava, Raghuvir Singh, Energy Management for Wireless Sensor Network Nodes, International Journal of Advances in Engineering & Technology, Vol. 1, Mar 2011

[5] Cardei, M.; Thai, M.T.; Yingshu Li; Weili Wu; Energy-Efficient Target Coverage in Wireless Sensor Networks, 24th Annual Joint Conference of the IEEE Computer and Communications Societies. INFOCOM 2005.

[6] Fuad Bajaber, Irfan Awan.: Adaptive decentralized re-clustering protocol for wireless sensor networks, Journal of computer and Systems sciences, doi:10.1016/j.jcss.2010.01.007.

[7] Yi-hua zhu, Wan-deng wu, Jian pan, Yi-ping tang.: An energy efficient data gathering algorithm to prolong lifetime of wireless sensor networks, Computer Communications 33, pp. 639-647 (2010).

[8] Fuad Bajaber, Irfan Awan.: Energy efficient clustering protocol to enhance lifetime of wireless sensor network, Journal of Ambient Intelligence and Human Computing 1, pp. 239-248 (2010).

[9] N.Dimokas, D.Katsaros,Y.Manolopoulos.: Energy-efficient distributed clustering in wireless sensor networks, Journal of Parallel and Distributed Computing 70, pp. 371-383 (2010).

[10] Jamal N. Al-Karaki, Raza Ul-Mustafa, Ahmed E. Kamal, "Data Aggregation in Wireless Sensor Networks - Exact and Approximate Algorithms'", Proceedings of IEEE Workshop on HighPerformance Switching and Routing (HPSR), USA.

Chapter 3. Secure Data Aggregation in Wireless Sensor Networks

3.1 Overview

Secure data aggregation is a highly exigent chore in wireless sensor networks. Our paper proposed a secure data aggregation based on clustering techniques using fuzzy logic. The performs the clustering and cluster head process in a network. Each cluster are calculated the distance, power consumed and faith value. Based on these parameters the secure data aggregation using fuzzy logic techniques. After the aggregated data send from the cluster heads to the base stations. Our proposed work has less energy consumption to prolonging the increasing the network life time in wireless sensor networks.

3.2 Introduction

Wireless Sensor Networks is one of the important technologies for twenty first century. The recent advances in MEMS and Wireless Communication technologies has a tiny, cheap and smart sensors through a wireless link for various civilian and military applications like environmental monitoring, battle field surveillance, and also industry process control. It also included the temperature, light, sound and humidity. A sensor networks is required fast and easy to install and maintain. Most of the network layer attacks against sensor networks into following categories like spoofed, altered, (or) replayed routing information, selective forwarding, sinkhole attacks, wormholes, HELLO flood attacks, Acknowledgement spoofing. Spoofed attacks a routing protocol is to target the routing information exchanged between nodes. The malicious nodes may refuse to forward certain message and ensuring not propagated will receives message for multi-hop networks.

3.3 Data Aggregation

Data gathering is one of the main objectives of sensor nodes. It involves collecting the sensed data from multiple sensors and transmitting the data to the base station. It is the process of aggregating the data from the multiple sensors to remove the redundant transmission information to the base station. The various issues into following categories like: 1. Some nodes to transmit the data directly to the base station have reduced energy. 2. The data aggregation for improving clustering techniques to conserved the energy of the sensors. It is also improve the energy efficiency.

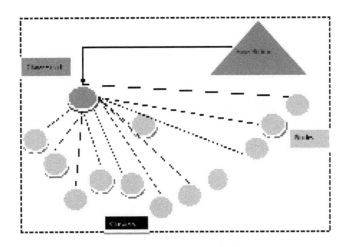

Figure 1: Data Aggregation in Wireless Sensor Networks

3.4 Attacks in WSN

Wormholes attack is a severe threat in wireless sensor networks. The packets from one location tunnels and replays to another location. Jamming attacks the sensor nodes using the radio frequencies causes the message are corrupted in a network. Modification attacks to change the data after send through the receiver. Denial of Service (DOS) attack attempt to computer resources in all layer of OSI model.

3.5 Proposed Work

The Sensor nodes are grouped various clusters and each clusters have elected as one cluster head with ID. The cluster head to calculate the distance between each member and also exchanged the topology to discover the packets. The cluster head collect the data from each member to calculate the power level by using the formula.

Power= Energy * Time

Finally the Fuzzy Logic is used to select the best nodes for aggregation. The Parameters like faith value, power level and distance from each node through cluster head as taken as input and fuzzy rules are formed. The rules are based on the output will be treated as the best node and worst node. The best nodes are aggregated with the cluster head ID, the data send to the base station. The Cluster Head ID is mentioned like the nodes are the best node in the network. The Remaining Worst nodes are eliminating in the network.

19

A. Distance Calculation

The Euclidean distance from each cluster head through the neighboring nodes (a,b) calculated by using the formula,

$$D = ((a_2-a_1)^2 + (b_2-b_1)^2))^{1/2}$$

B. Energy Calculation

The Energy calculated by using the formula in a network,

$$E_{total} = E_{tx} + E_{rx} + E_{intial} + E_{sensing}$$

Where,

E_{total}- Total energy cost in a network

E_{tx}-Transmitter cost

E_{rx}-Receiver cost

E_{intial}- Idle energy cost in a network

$E_{sensing}$- sensing node energy cost

C. Fuzzy Logic

The degree of the input fundamental steps and condition of fuzzy logic are strong-minded. On the basis of the rule is gritty. The results are acquired every fuzzy rules are multiple together with single overall results. The fuzzy sets of A with a membership function of X rules are determined. Antecedent 1 and 2 are the low the consequent are high.

$$\text{Distance (D)} = \{ [BN, a], [WN, b] \}$$

Where,

a-Fuzzy set membership grade Best Node in Cluster ID with distance calculation

b-Fuzzy set membership grade Worst Node in Cluster ID with distance calculation

$$\text{Power Consumed (P)} = \{ [BN, c], [WN, d] \}$$

Where,

c-Fuzzy set membership grade Best Node in Cluster ID with power consumption

d-Fuzzy set membership grade Worst Node in Cluster ID with power consumption

$$\text{Faith Value (F)} = \{ [BN, e], [WN, f] \}$$

Where,

e-Fuzzy set membership grade Best Node in Cluster ID with faith value

f-Fuzzy set membership grade Worst Node in Cluster ID with faith value

Table 1: Decision Making using Fuzzy Logic Techniques

Distance D	Power Consumed P	Faith Value F	Consequences
Low	Low	High	Best
Low	High	High	Best
High	Low	Less	Best
Low	Low	Less	Best
High	High	Less	Worst
High	Low	Less	Worst
Low	High	Less	Worst
High	High	High	Worst

3.6 Results and Discussion

Nodes have been transmitted at a specified interval one after another. Figure 2 show that the clustering techniques transmitted data to the base stations. Figure 3 shows that the Throughput in secured data aggregation using Fuzzy Logic techniques.

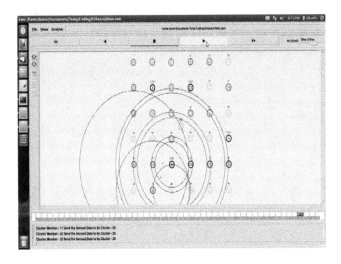

Figure 2: Clustering techniques transmitted data to the base station

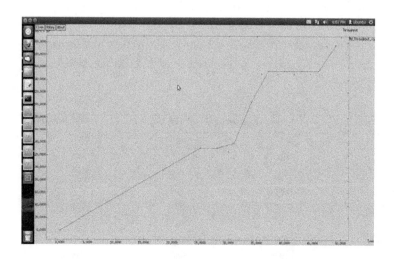

Figure 3: Throughput in Secured data aggregation using Fuzzy Logic

3.7 Conclusion

The Sensor Nodes have higher signal strength are elected as cluster heads. The parameters are distance, Power consumed and faith value of sensor nodes can be used as data aggregation. The fuzzy logic consider as the best node and worst node. After the classification the best node are selected as data aggregation then the worst node are neglected by cluster head. By simulated the results our technique has superior the throughput with condensed packet drop and also a lesser amount of energy consumption. The results are proved the effectiveness of our proposed techniques.

References

[1] B.Baranidharan, B.Shanthi, "A New Graph Theory based Routing Protocol for Wireless Sensor Networks", International journal on applications of graph theory in wireless ad hoc networks and sensor networks (GRAPH-HOC) Vol.3, No.4, December 2011

[2] S. Swapna Kumar , M. Nanda Kumar, V. S. Sheeba ,K. R. Kashwan" Cluster Based Routing Algorithm Using Dual Staged Fuzzy Logic in Wireless Sensor Networks" Journal of Information & Computational Science 9: 5 (2012) 1281–1297 Available at http://www.joics.com

[3] Ashutosh Kumar Singh, Sandeep Goutele, S.Verma and N. Purohit , " An Energy Efficient Approach for Clustering in WSN using Fuzzy Logic" International Journal of Computer Applications (0975 – 8887) Volume 44– No18, April 2012

[4] Q. Liang, "Clusterhead election for mobile ad hoc wireless network," in Proc. 14th IEEE International Symposium on Personal, Indoor and Mobile Radio Communications, (PIMRC) , pp. 1623 -1628, Sept. 2003.

[5] Indranil Gupta, Denis Riordan and Srinivas Sampalli, "Cluster-head Election using Fuzzy Logic for Wireless Sensor Networks", the 3rd Annual Communication Networks and Services Research Conference (CNSR'05), pp. 255 - 260, 2005.

[6] Jong-Myoung Kim, Seon-Ho Park, Young-Ju Han and Tai-Myoung Chung, "CHEF: Cluster Head Election mechanism using Fuzzy logic in Wireless Sensor Networks", Advanced Communication Technology, 2008. ICACT 2008. 10th International Conference, pp. 654 – 659, vol. 1, 2008.

[7] Junpei Annoa, Leonard Barollib, Arjan Durresic, Fatos Xhafad and Akio Koyamae, "Performance evaluation of two fuzzy-based cluster head selection systems for wireless sensor networks", Network-Based Information Systems (NBiS), 2010 13th International Conference pp. 55-61, 2010.

[8] Ning Sun, Nai-bin Su and Sang-ho Lee, "A Lifetime Extended Routing Protocol Based on Data Threshold in Wireless Sensor Networks", 10th IEEE International Conference on Computer and Information Technology (CIT 2010), pp. 743-748, 2010.

[9] Rong Ding, Bing Yang, Lei Yang and Jiawei Wang, "Soft Threshold Based Cluster-head Selection Algorithm for Wireless Sensor Networks", Third International Conference on Sensor Technologies and Applications, pp. 526-530, 2009.

[10] Nasrin Abazari Torghabeh, Mohammad Reza Akbarzadeh Totonchi and Mohammad Hossein Yaghmaee Moghaddam, "Cluster Head Selection using a Two-Level Fuzzy Logic in Wireless Sensor Networks", Computer Engineering and Technology (ICCET), 2010 2nd International Conference, pp. 357-361, vol. 2, 2010.

[11] Hironori Ando, Leonard Barolli, Arjan Durresi, Fatos Xhafa, and Akio Koyama, "An Intelligent Fuzzy-based Cluster Head Selection System for Wireless Sensor Networks and Its Performance Evaluation", 13th International Conference on Network-Based Information Systems, pp. 55-61, 2010.

[12] Hironori Ando, Leonard Barolli, Arjan Durresi, Fatos Xhafa, and Akio Koyama, "An Intelligent Fuzzy-based Cluster Head Selection System for WSNs and ItsPerformance Evaluation for D3N Parameter", International Conference on Broadband, Wireless Computing, Communication and Applications, pp. 648-653, 2010.

[13] Sudakshina Dasgupta and Paramartha Dutta, "An improved Leach approach for Head selection Strategy in a Fuzzy-C Means induced clustering of a Wireless Sensor Network", IEMCON 2011 organised by IEM in collaboration with IEEE on 5th & 6th of Jan,2011, pp. 203-208, 2010.

[14] Xiao Fu and Zhenhua Yu, "A Reliable and Efficient Clustering Algorithm for Wireless Sensor Networks Using Fuzzy Petri Nets", Wireless Communications Networking and Mobile Computing (WiCOM), 2010 6th International Conference, pp. 1-4, 2010.

[15] A. Manjeshwar; D.P. Agrawal, "TEEN : A routing protocol for enhanced efficiency in wireless sensor networks", 15th International Parallel and Distributed Processing Symposium, pp.2009-2015, Apr 2001.

[16] N.Eshghi and A.T.Haghighat,"Energy Conservation Strategy in Clusterbased Wireless Sensor Network", IEEE ICACTE, pp.1015- 1019, 2008

Chapter 4- P-Persistent Access Protocol in Wireless Sensor Networks

4.1 Overview

In the world of computers, networking is the practice of linking two or more computing devices together for the purpose of sharing data. Networks are built with a mix of computer hardware and software. Networking includes communication with other uses, centralization of software and account maintenance and mobility of uses. Whenever there is more than one computer being used as the same location networking them together makes a lot of sense. Not only can the file transferred between them quickly and easily, but they can also share expensive resources like laser printers, hard disc arrays, backup tape drives, CD and DVD burners, scanners, internet connection and so on.

Sharing of files from source to the destination is often referred as file sharing, in networking. The router is the primary component, which is used to transfer all such files. While transferring the files these routers are compromised by the attackers and hence it becomes malicious in nature. Therefore there arrives a problem in the delivery of files, because of this malicious router. So I am in detecting the existence of compromised routers and isolate them from the routing fabric by using the mobile agents called as Ant Nets.

Wireless technology has enabled has enabled the development of increasingly diverse applications and devices resulting in an exponential growth in usage and services. This advancement made the radiofrequency spectrum a scarce resource, and consequently, its efficient use is of the ultimate importance. Cognitive radio can reduce the spectrum shortage problem by enabling unlicensed users equipment with cognitive radio to reuse and share the licensed spectrum bands. Firstly, prediction techniques are evaluated and compared for prediction accuracy. Secondly, routing protocol reliability, efficiency and scalability performance improvements even with moderate accuracy predictors. Results clearly show that hybrid markov CDF prediction performs the best. When compared with no prediction it significantly improves average reliability and efficiency by11% and 8% respectively

4.2 Introduction

During the last decade, Wavelength Division Multiplexing (WDM) Networks have emerged as on attractive architecture for backbone networks [1]. WDM networks provide high band width, on the order of tens of gigabits per second per channel. In, recently two observations are driving the research community to explore the traffic grooming problem in WDM networks. First, the bandwidth requirements of most of the current applications are just a fraction of the band width offered by a single wavelength in WDM networks. Second, the dominant cost factor in WDM networks is not the number of wavelengths but rather the network components, specifically, higher layer equipment, such as SONET Add/Drop multiplexers (ADMs), or MPLS or IP router ports [2].

The cost effectiveness of WDM Networks depends on the amount of the wireless pass-through provided by the network to the given traffic, thus reducing the number and cost of the higher layer equipment [3]. At, the amount of the wireless pass-through depends on the traffic arrangement on the wireless layer. Traffic grooming is therefore defined as an intelligent allocation of the traffic demands, in different networks notes, on to an available set of wavelengths in such a way the reduces the overall cost of the network. In general the traffic grooming problem is recorded to be even harder than the combined virtual topology design and routing and wavelength assignment (RWA) [4].

To make the problem somewhat less difficult, many relaxations have been considered in the literature [5]. For example, most of the studies allow the traffic of each source-destination set to be (vertically) split over multiple wavelengths-a condition known as bifurcation. Due to bifurcation different components of the same traffic dement may traverse different links. This provision provides flexibility in traffic allocation, which may lead to a reduction in the number of wavelengths as he uses number of ADMs [6].

4.3 Proposed Work

During the past few years, cognitive radio networks (CRNs) have emerged as a solution for the problems created due to fixed spectrum allocation such as inefficient usage of licensed spectrum. CRNs aim at solving this problem by exploiting the spectrum holes (the spectrum not being used by primary radio nodes at a particular time) and allocation the spectrum dynamically. In this paper, we address the problem of dynamic channel assignment for cognitive radio users in multi-radio multichannel cognitive radio network (MRMC-CRNs). We propose an efficient spectrum-aware dynamic channel assignment (SA-DCA) with two related strategies. Simulation results show that SA-DCA with two related in signification reduced interference to primary radio nodes increased packet delivery ration in MRMC-CRNs.

Spectrum sharing has attention in cognitive radio recently as an efficient of alleviating the spectrum scarcity problem by allowing unlicensed users to coexist with licensed under the condition of protecting the latter from harmful interference. In this paper, few focus kin the condition of protecting the latter from harmful interference. In this paper, we focus on the through put maximization of spectrum sharing cognitive radio networks and propose a novel cognitive radio system that significantly improves their achievable throughput.

More specifically, we introduce a novel receiver and frame structure for spectrum sharing cognitive radio networks and study the problem of deriving the optimal power allocation strategy that maximizes the ergodic capacity of the proposed cognitive radio system under average transmit and interference power constraints. In addition, we study the outage capacity of the proposed cognitive radio system under various constraints that include average transmit and interference power constraints, and peak interference power constraints. Finally we provide simulation results, in order to demonstrate the improved ergodic and outage throughput achieved by the proposed cognitive radio system compared to conventional spectrum sharing cognitive radio systems.

.   With the rapid proliferation of new technologies and services in the wireless domain, scarcity has become a major concern. The allocation of the industrial, Medical and scientific (ISM) band has enabled the explosion of new technologies (e.g. WI-FI) due to its license-exempt characteristic. The widespread adoption of WI-FI technology, combined with the rapid penetration of smart phones running popular user service (e.g. social online networks) has overcrowded substantially the ISM band. On the other hand according to a number of recent reports, several parts of the static allocated licensed bands are under-utilized. This has brought up the idea of the opportunistic use of these bands, so called, cognitive radio and cognitive radio networks. Security threats are mainly related to two fundamental characteristics of cognitive radios: cognitive capability, and reconfigurability. Furthermore, as cognitive wireless networks. The scope of this work is to give an overview face, along with the current state-of-the art to detect the corresponding attacks. In addition, future challenges are addressed.

In this paper, we present an analytical framework to evaluate the latency performance of connection-based spectrum handoffs in cognitive radio (CR) networks. During the transmission period of a secondary connection, multiple interruption from the primary users result in multiple spectrum handoffs. To quantity the effects of channel obsolete issue on the target channel predetermining a set of target channel predetermination, we should consider the three key design features:

1. General service time distribution of the primary and secondary connection;
2. Different operating channels in multiple handoffs; and
3. Queuing delay due to channel contention from multiple secondary connections.

Cognitive radio (CR) is the enabling technology for supporting dynamic spectrum access: the policy that addresses the spectrum scarcity problem that addresses the spectrum scarcity problem that is encountered in many counties. To make radio and wireless networks truly cognitive, however, is by no means a simple task, and it requires collaborative effort from various research communities, including communications theory, networking engineering, signal processing, game theory.

4.4 Proposed Markov Chain Implementation

We model the channel search and access policy for a CRN containing one SU by on open network. It will be extended to the multiuser case in the next sections. The networking is compressed of several nodes corresponding to different stages of spectrum sensing and packet transmission attempt of pack including channel sensing and packet transmission. In the proposed model, the arrival of a request to the queuing network presents the transmission attempt of a packet including channel sensing and handovers. The request leaves the network after in the service from a subset of nodes. Different handovers are modeled through nodes Hoi, i=1, 2... $, where $ is the maximum number of allowed handovers and will be discussed later. It is worth nothing that the first handover node does not really exist in the process of finding a transmission opportunity, and it appears just for providing symmetry in the model. Let Si denote the sensing process of ith channel. At the beginning of each time slot, an SU's request enters the node HO1, and immediately is routed to the first sensing node, S!. After time units, the channel sensor routes the request to the transmitter nodes (node T*LPI or T*HP1) or to the second handover nod, HO2.

Let as defined the ith stage of the sensing-transmission process, as the set of nodes Hoi, Si, T*HPi. At the ith stage, the ith channel is sensed free if (a) the ith PU is absence (with the probability of pi ,o) and the SU correctly detects this transmission opportunity, with the probability of Pi,0(1_pfa,i), or (b) the channel is occupied by the PU(with probability of Pi,1=1_pi,0) but the SU mistakenly senses this channel free, with the probability of Pi,1 (1_Pd,i), where Pfa, I and pd, I denote the false alarm and detection probabilities of the sensing process of the ith channel. Please note that similar, in this study, we evaluate the SUs performance while their impacts on the Pus communications are limited, i.e., the admissible false alarm and miss detection probabilities are restricted according to the IEEE 802.22 standard. Hence, the desired Q0s of the Pus is provided. Nodes T*HPi model the first case in which the Su will be able to transmit on the ith channel for the rest of the time slot with the capacity of c0 = log2 (1+s). In the same way, in nodes T*LPi which models the later case (case b), the SU will be to transmit on the ith channel for the time slot with the capacity.

4.5 Modified P-Persistent Access Protocol

We extend the considered sequential approach by modifying the queue network to include the multiuser SRN. In order to provide multiple accesses among the SUs, a modified version of the conventional p-persistent multiple access protocol is utilized in which each Su sense each channel with the probability p and skips the sensing process with the probability (1-p). The channel sensing probability, p, provides a degree of freedom to optimize the performance matrices, namely, throughput of SUs. The channel sensing access policy of the proposed modified p-persistent access protocol (MPPA) used by each SU. Since at each stage I some requests may not be routed to the node Si, in order to synchronize the results. More specifically, the requests that enter standby mode (at node SY Ni) wait for time units (sensing period).

The same procedure told in the paper is enhanced for general network switching is so called Handoff/ Handover. When We Exit and Enter from One Network to another Network we are supposed to change the network criteria due to the network where we are going to mo. So in this project we are going to implement the Handoff/ handover technique from one network to the other network.

4.6 P-Persistent Random Access

The major disadvantage associated with the MPPA algorithm is that a high number of SUs (pNp SUs) intend to sense the first channel through the node s1. Similarly, the c1Np SUs to exploit the spectrum resources in each stage and consequently degrade the performance regarding the average SUs' throughput. In order to mitigate the aforementioned problem, we consider the p-persistent random access (PPRA) scheme, which equally distributes level and raises the throughput of each SU. Demonstrates the sensing-transmission stages of the proposed PPRA method.

4.7 Spectrum Sensing Using Multiple Nodes

When the CR RX is equipped with multiple antennas, Eigen value-based detection (EBD) can be used for spectrum sensing. By constructing the sample covariance matrix of the received signals, EBD simultaneously estimates the noise variance and signal power by calculating the minimum and maximum Eigen values of the matrix. When the primary signal is activate and the signal covariance matrix is not a scalar of the identity matrix, the difference between these two Eigen values are supposed to be the same however, when the primary signal is activate ND the signal covariance matrix is not a scalar of the identity matrix, the difference between the two Eigen values expected to larger. Thus the condition number of the sample covariance matrix can be used as the test statistics for signal detection. A closed-form formula for the probability density function of the test statistic can be derived by using a random matrix theory, through which he detection threshold can be determined for a target probability of false alarm.

Because EBD simultaneously estimates the noise variance and signal power, it tends to be noise power uncertainty. In, it is shown that EBD has a theoretical root in generalized likelihood radio testing, from which other versions of sensing algorithms can be developed. For example, the testing statistic can be chosen at the ratio of the arithmetic mean over the geometric mean of the Eigen values of the sample covariance matrix. On the other hand, if the noise variance is known to the CX< RX< the maximum Eigen values can be used as the test statistics.

4.8. Cognitive Spectrum Access

Spectrum-sensing techniques for identifying the spectrum holes have been received from the signal processing perspective. Based on the sensing results, the CR users can perform cognitive spectrum access through the OSA model. Alternatively, If the CR TX has obtained the channel-state information involved for primary RX protection, the CSA model can be used for cognitive spectrum access. In particular, transmit signal waveform design is considered do the OSA model, and transmit and resource allocation is studied for the CSA model. The capacity limits of CR channels with genie cognitive capability have been considered from the information-theoretic perspective. The transmit strategies for the CSA model are also reviewed in the convex optimization perspective, as well as, with additional consideration of cooperative communications.

In OSA, multicarrier modulation techniques become natural candidates for CR transmission mainly due to flexibility in spectrum usage. As the most popular multicarrier technique, OFDM, with its own advantages of combating fading and interface, has been proposed for the PHY layer of CR. OFDM-based spectrum pooling has extensively been discussed in, where several potential identified, among which the mutual interference between the CR uses and the Pus is critical for CR users to work on a noninterference basis. Windowing and active subcarrier cancelation techniques have been proposed to reduce the power leakage in the side lobes of OFDM subcarriers to limit the interference level.

4.10. Spectrum-Aware Routing

The stability aware routing protocol (STRAP) has been developed for multichip DSA networks and can utilize unused frequency bands without compromising the stability of the network. Another proposal is the spectrum aware routing protocol (SPEAR), which can establish robust paths even in the diverse spectrum environment with rather stringent latency condition spectrum aware on demand routing for CRNs, was also considered by cheng. Where the routing and spectrum allocation algorithm is one of the recent proposals for enabling throughput maximization in this context, taking care of the interference minimization and maximizing the weighted sum of differential backlogs so that system stays stable. See a related work in and the reference therein.

4.9 Results and Discussion

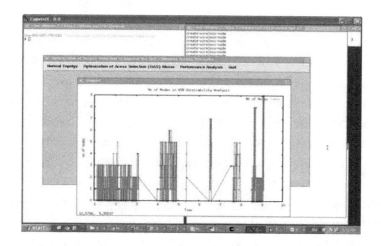

Figure 1: Number of Nodes in WSN

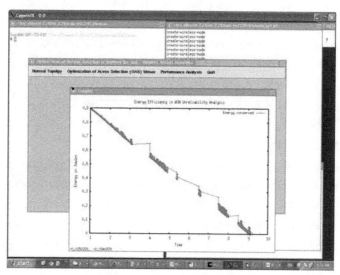

Figure 2: Energy Effiiency in WSN

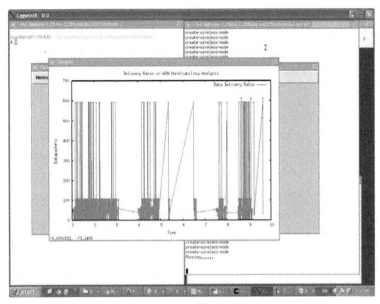

Figure 3: Delivery Ratio in WSN

4.11 Conclusion

The main result in this paper is that, under tight collision constraints, optimal cognitive access of multiple continuous tiles on off morkovien channels can be achieved by deterministic periodic sensing randomized transmission policies designing, modeling and systematic performance evaluating of channel sensing schemes in a multichannel cognitive radio networks (CRNs) have been investigated. Modified p-persistent access (MPPA) has been introduced and its performance in terms of the average SUs' throughput and the average number of handovers has been evaluated. In order to appropriately mitigate the problem associated with the MPPA scheme, a distributed sensing access policy, called p-persistent random access (PPRA), has been proposed, which statistically distributes the SUs' load among the channels and offers higher average throughput.

References

1. A survey on security threats and detection techniques in cognitive radio networks (2013) fragkiadakis.A.G, tragos.E.Z, Askoxyylakis.I.G.

2. Enhancing the capacity of spectrum sharing cognitive radio networks stotas., Nallanathan.A.

3. Impact of mobility prediction on the performance of Cognitive Radio networks (2010) Butun. I Cagatay Talay. A, Altilar.D.T, Khalid.Murad, Sankar. Ravi.

4. Modeling and analysis for spectrum handoffs in cognitive radio network (2014) L.C.Wang, C.W.Wang, and C.J.Chang

5. Cognitive radio networking and communications: an overview (2011) Y,-c. Liang. K.C. Chen, Y, Li, and P.Mahonen.

6. I.F.Akyildiz,W.Su,Y.Sankarasubramaniam,E.Cayirci,"Wireless sensor Networks: A Survey",Computer Networks (Elseveir) 393–422,2002

7. Chris Karlof, David Wagner, "Secure routing in wireless sensor networks: Attacks and Countermeasures", Special issue on sensor network application protocols, 2003

8. P.Papadimitratos and Z.J.Haas, "Secure routing for mobile ad hoc networks", In Proceedings of the SCS Communication Networks and Distributed Systems Modeling and Simulation Conference (CNDS 2002), January, 2002

9. Majid meghdadi, Suat ozdemir, Inan giller, "A Survey on wormhole based attacks and their countermeasures in wireless sensor networks", IETE Technical Review, VOL 28, ISSUE 2, 2011

10. Y. C. Hu, A. Perrig, and D.B. Johnson, "Packet leashes: a defense against wormhole attacks in wireless networks", Conference of the IEEE Computer and Communications Societies (INFOCOM),pp. 1976-1986, 2003.

11. R. Poovendran and L. Lazos, "A graph theoretic framework for preventing the wormhole attack in wireless ad hoc networks", ACM Journal of Wireless Networks(WINET), 2005.

12. Maheshwari R, Gao Jie, Das S R. "Detecting wormhole attacks in wireless networks using connectivity information", IEEE International Conference on Computer Communications, 2007:107-115.

13. Hu Y C, Perrig A, Johnson D. "Wormhole attacks in wireless networks", IEEE J. Sel. Areas Communication, 2006.

14. S.Capkun,L. Buttyán, and J.-P. Hubaux, "SECTOR: Secure Tracking of Node Encounters in Multi-hop Wireless Networks", ACM workshop on Security of adhoc and sensor networks (SASN 03), pp.21-32, 2003.

15. Hu Lingxuan, Evans D, "Using directional antennas to prevent wormhole attacks", In Network and distributed network security symposium, 2004

16. Alzaid, Hani and Abanmi, Suhail and Kanhere, Salil and Chou, Chun Tung "Detecting Wormhole Attacks in Wireless Sensor Networks". Technical Report,2006

17. Khalil I, Bagchi S, Shroff N B, "Liteworp: Detection and isolation of the wormhole attack in static multihop wireless networks", Computer Networks 2007,**51**(13):3750-3772.

18. Khalil I, Bagchi S, Shroff N B. "Mobiworp: Mitigation of the wormhole attack in mobile multihop wireless networks", Ad Hoc Networks 2008, **6**(3): 344-362.

Chapter 5- Graph Theory in Wireless Sensor Networks

5.1 Overview

Wireless Sensor Networks (WSN) have become a critical research issue for a wide range of applications such as environmental monitoring, medical, habitat monitoring, surveillance and tracking systems with the improvement of wireless communication and VLSI technology.WSN is consisted of a large number of sensor nodes to collect the information and dispatch information. . As power is a limiting factor in a WSN, the major challenge in deploying a WSN is to enhance the network life time. So, it becomes inevitable to devise an efficient method of conserving the power. Wireless Sensor Networks have many nodes are connected to the network to calculate the network performance like transmission power. The power consumption is directly related to the size and weight of the nodes. It gains low cost and also to detect shortest path to transmitted the power through the network. The major design challenge for WSN is to extend the lifetime of sensor nodes longer and reduce power consumption important issue to prolong the lifetime of WSN.

5.2 Introduction

Wireless sensor networks (WSNs) have become a hot research topic in recent years. Wireless sensor network is one of the pervasive networks which sense our environment through various parameters like heat, temperature, pressure, etc... [1]Since sensor networks are based on the dense deployment of disposable and low-cost sensor nodes, destruction of some nodes by hostile action does not affect a military operation as much as the destruction of a traditional sensor, which makes the sensor network concept a better approach for battlefields. [2]. The transmission between the two nodes will minimize the other nodes to show the improve throughput and greater than spatial reuse than wireless networks to lack the power controls. Transmission Power technique to improve the Network Life Time in Wireless Sensor Networks [3]. Wireless sensor networks (WSNs) are emerging as an effective means for environment monitoring to improve the quality of life and safety in emergency situations. Sensor networks are equipped with energy limited batteries; energy conservation in such networks is prolonging the network lifetime. Advances in wireless sensor network (WSN) technology has provided the various types of physical and environmental conditions, data processing, and wireless communication and the characteristics of wireless sensor networks require more effective methods for data forwarding and processing.

5.3 Graph Theory

Graph theoretical ideas are highly research areas of computer science such data mining, image segmentation, clustering, image capturing, networking etc., Modeling of network topologies can be done using graph concepts. The shortest spanning tree in a weighted graph, obtaining an optimal match of nodes and distance and locating the shortest path between two vertices in a graph.

Some algorithms are as follows:

1. Shortest path algorithm in a network

 2. Finding a minimum spanning tree

3. Finding graph planarity

4. Algorithms to find adjacency matrices.

5. Algorithms to find the connectedness

6. Algorithms to find the cycles in a graph

7. Algorithms for searching an element in a data structure (DFS, BFS) and so on.

5.4 Related Work

Many algorithms and techniques have been developed that utilize power in an efficient manner. Some of the techniques and methods that are used to design the proposed algorithm are discussed here to know how power is dynamically reconciled to meet the constraint of power depletion in nodes of the network.

Sorooshyari et.al. have addressed the problem of adjusting the transmission power level at each wireless radio interface on a per packet basis, based on user and network applications. They have put forth a power control policy that enables a user to address various user – centric and network – centric objectives. The proposed power control policy is optimal with respect to users dynamically allocating transmit power.

Correia et. al. in have devised two transmission power control protocols for WSNs, which can be embedded into any existing MAC protocol. The first, called Hybrid, calculates the ideal transmission power using a closed control loop that iterates over the available transmissions powers in order to maintain a target link quality. The second, called AEWMA, employs calculations to determine the ideal transmission power based on the reception transmission power and average noise.

Arnab Nandi et. al. have propose power based transmission scheme for WSN where transmit power is adapted depending on node density and channel conditions so as to maintain a desired level of signal detection probability at a receiving node as demanded by sensing range. They have compared the energy level performance and the proposed transmit power schemes. With respect to energy consumption, they have shown that the proposed scheme consumes less energy than FTPS in moderate and high node spatial density region.

Jasmine Norman in their paper have developed Random Geometric Graphs a very influential and well-studied model of large networks, such as sensor networks, where the network nodes are represented by the vertices of the RGG, and the direct connectivity between nodes is represented by the edges. This assumes homogeneous wireless nodes with uniform transmission ranges. In real life, there exist heterogeneous wireless networks in which devices have dramatically different capabilities. The connectivity of a WSN is related to the positions of nodes, and those positions are heavily affected by the method of sensor deployment. As sensors may be spread in an arbitrary manner, one of the fundamental issues in a wireless sensor network is the coverage problem. study connectivity and coverage in hybrid WSN based on dynamic random geometric graph.

B.Baranidharan in their paper have energy efficiency in wireless sensor network [WSNs] is the highly sorted area for the researchers. Number of protocols has been suggested for energy efficient information gathering for sensor networks. These protocols come under two broad categories called tree based approach and clustering techniques. In these techniques clustering is more suitable for real time applications and has much more scalability factor when compared with its previous counterpart. It presents the importance and factors affecting the clustering. Surveyed the different clustering algorithms with its extensions till date and proposed the clustering technique using Minimum Spanning Tree [MST] and shortest path concept with its strength and limitations.

5.5 Proposed Work

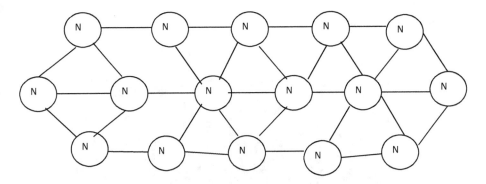

Figure 1: Network Structure

The main objective of the paper is to develop a transmission power technique using graph approach. The Graph based Transmission Power is developed to prolong the lifetime of WSN by reducing the communication mechanism with reduced processing and network power consumption. The basic ideology behind this novel method is to reduce the transmission power of the node automatically so that the communication happens on a one to one basis. The concept of the transmission technique is best implemented with Graph Theory. In Graph Theory, the nodes are treated as vertices and the links between them are considered as edges of the graph. Consider the network shown in Figure 1.

The sensors are deployed randomly in a WSN. The distance between the sensors nodes need to be calculated to know the neighboring nodes of a particular node. Calculating the distance from the node also helps in finding the amount of power required to reach the next neighbor node. Network nodes are represented by the vertices and also direct connectivity between the nodes by the edges. Sensor nodes are maximum flow from one node to the other node to calculate the distance. The Combinatorial Structure is called as network structure. The Number of vertices are connected to the source node in a network is called its neighbor node and the number of edges are its size. Two or more edges of a network joining the same pair of vertices are called multiple edges. The distance calculation and the neighborhood discovery form the basis for finding the shortest path that can be taken to communicate between the source and the destination with reduced power requirement thereby prolonging the life time of the network.

5.6. Result and Discussion

Figure 2: Node Result

Figure 2 shows the Number of nodes results in the given network of the wireless sensor networks.

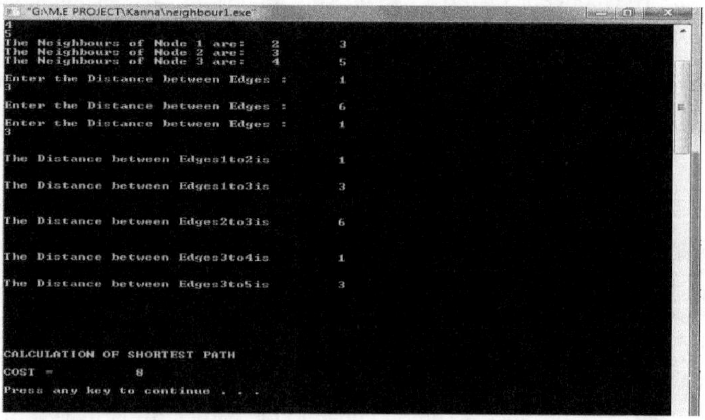

Figure 3: Shortest Path Result

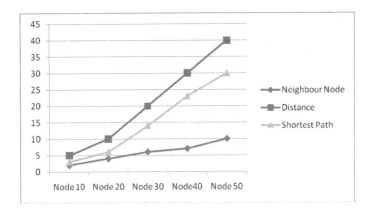

Figure 4: Comparison of Various Nodes

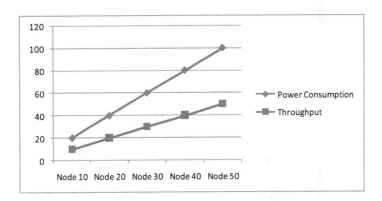

Figure 5: Power Consumption of various Nodes

Figure 3 shows that shortest path of given network based on the distance of the neighboring node. Figure 4 shows the comparison of various node based on the distance, shortest path and neighboring node of the given network. Figure 5 shows that power consumption of various nodes.

5.7 Conclusion

The proposed system of Transmission power technique is to enhance the lifetime of the entire sensor network. The eligible sensor nodes are chosen depending on their power levels and association with number of nodes in transmission area. The efficiency of the proposed model is experimented and evaluated in C++ and the results accomplished showed that in this technique, sensor nodes utilize extremely less power and stay in the network for a greater period of time.

References

[1] Sorooshyari. S, Gajic Z, "Autonomous Dynamic Power Control for Wireless Networks: User-centric and Network centric consideration", IEEE Trans. On Wireless Communications. Vol. 7, Issue 3. Pp 1004-1015. March 2008.

[2] Correia L.T.H.A., Macedo D.F., Silva D.A.C., Santos A.L.D., Loureiro A.A.F. and Noguerira J.M.S., "Transmission Power Control in MAC Protocols for Wireless Sensor Networks", Proc. of the 8th ACM/IEEE International Symposium on Modelling, Analysis and Simulation of Wireless and Mobile Systems (MSWiM'05), Montreal, Quebec, Canada, 2005. Pp 282- 289.

[3] Arnab Nandi, Sumit Kundu "On Energy Level Performance of Adaptive Power Based WSN in Presence of Fading" , International Journal of Energy, Information and Communications Vol. 3, Issue 2, May, 2012.

[4] Khemapech I., Miller A. and Duncan I., "A Survey of Transmission Power Control in Wireless Sensor Networks", Proc. of the 8th Annual Postgraduate symposium on the Convergence of Telecommunications, Networking and Broadcasting (PGNet 2007). 2007. Pp. 15-20.

[5] Pantazis N.A., Vergados D.D., Miridakis N.I. and Vergados D.J., "Power control schemes in wireless sensor networks for homecare e-health applications", ACM International Conference Proceeding Series, Athens, Greece, 2008.

[6] Kayhan Erciyes , Orhan Dagdeviren , Deniz Cokuslu , Deniz Ozsoyeller, "Graph Theoretic Clustering Algorithms in Mobile Ad hoc Networks and Wireless Sensor Networks - Survey", Appl. Comput. Math. 6 (2007), no.2, pp.162-180.

[7] Jin Wang, Tinghuai Ma, Qi Liu, Sai Ji, Sungyoung Lee, "A Novel Transmission Power Control Approach for Wireless Sensor Networks", Sensor Letters, 2012

[8] Martin Kubisch, Holger Karl, Adam Wolisz, Lizhi Charlie Zhong, Jan Rabaey, "Distributed Algorithms for Transmission Power Control in Wireless Sensor Networks", proceeding of: IEEE Wireless Communications and Networking, 2003

[9] Christopher Grin, "Graph Theory" Penn State Math 485 Lecture Notes Version 1.1, 2011-2012

[10] Monika Bathla, Nitin Sharma, "A Review Paper on Topology Control in Wireless Sensor Networks" IJECT Vol. 2, Issue 2, June 2011

[11] Suman Banerjee, Archan Misra, "Adapting Transmission Power for Optimal Energy Reliable Multi-hop Wireless Communication", Wireless Optimization Workshop (WiOpt'03), Sophia-Antipolis, France, March 2003.

[12] Niranjan Kumar Ray, Ashok Kumar Turuk, "Energy Efficient Techniques for Wireless Ad Hoc Network",

[13] Shan Lin, Jingbin Zhang, Gang Zhou, Lin Gu, Tian He, and John A. Stankovic,"ATPC: Adaptive Transmission Power Control for Wireless Sensor Networks", SenSys '06 Proceedings of the 4th international conference on Embedded networked sensor systems, Pages 223-236

[14] S.G.Shirinivas, S.Vetrivel, N.M.Elango "Applications of Graph Theory in Computer Science - An Overview", International Journal of Engineering Science and Technology, Vol. 2(9), 2010, 4610-4621

[15] Connectivity and Coverage in Hybrid Wireless Sensor Networks using Dynamic Random Geometric Graph Model, Author : Jasmine Norman, Vellore Institute of Technology, Vellore – 14, International journal on applications of graph theory in wireless ad hoc networks and sensor networks (GRAPH-HOC) Vol.3, No.3, September 2011 .

[16] A New Graph Theory based Routing Protocol for Wireless Sensor Networks, Author : B.Baranidharan, B.Shanthi, SASTRA University, School of Computing, Thanjavur, India, International journal on applications of graph theory in wireless ad hoc networks and sensor networks (GRAPH-HOC) Vol.3, No.4, December 2011.

[17] Bhupendra Gupta , Srikanth K Iyer , D Manjunath , "Topological Properties Of The One Dimensional Exponential Random Geometric Graph", Random Structures & Algorithms , Volume 32 , Issue 2 , 2008, pp: 181-204

[18] Chen Avin , "Random Geometric Graphs: An Algorithmic Perspective" , Ph,D dissertation, University of California , Los Angeles , 2006

[19] Chi-Fu Huang, Yu-Chee Tseng , "The Coverage Problem in a Wireless Sensor Network" , WSNA'03,September 19, 2003, San Diego, California, USA.

[20] J. Diaz D. Mitsche X. Pierez-Gimienez , "On the Connectivity of Dynamic Random Geometric Graphs, Symposium on Discrete Algorithms" , Proceedings of the nineteenth annual ACM-SIAM symposium on Discrete algorithms , 2008, pp 601-610

Chapter 6- Algorithm in Wireless Sensor Networks

6.1 Overview

The Networks are showing increasing into the number of Security threats in the wireless sensor networks. In this paper we have the energy efficient for different keys are generated as the purpose of security with encryption and decryption using the DES and RSA Algorithm is applied to the network. The channel quality is determined in wireless sensor networks. The different keys are generated to be secured data will send through the networks then the life time of the network is increased in the wireless sensor networks. Finally we analysis results using DES and RSA algorithm the given data are converted into encrypted and decrypted into the network to efficient the data secured. Our paper is done by using C++ simulation.

6.2 Introduction

Wireless Sensor Networks is a composed of number of sensor nodes in a large number of application such as military, airspace, temperature, light , humidity and then communicate with each sensor in wireless networks[1]. In the Wireless sensor networks cannot replace or recharge the batteries compared to the adhoc networks. So energy conservations are an important factor in wireless sensor networks [2]. Therefore the designing the network structure in an efficient way to the increasing the life of the networks in wireless sensor networks. The challenges in the network system included as Limited Hardware, Limited support for networking and also the Limited support for software development [3].

6.3 Security Threads

Internet are growing a large of threat are affectation continue reliability in the Denial of Service (dos) attacks. Such attacks can occur at all levels in the protocol stack and threaten both routers and hosts. Data confidentiality is important issues related to the security [4]. The data transferred towards the passive attacks are very sensitive to the data confidentiality. It can maintain confidentiality using cryptography techniques in the complex way encryption and decryption process involved into public key based generation have a power consumes are at higher rate [5]. In the sensor network a maximum number of the attacks are involved in the network layer are given as follows like Active attacks, Passive attacks, Wormhole attacks, Sinkhole attacks, Sybil attacks etc..

6.4 Network Structure

The Figure shows that of the given data are transferred to the network to be secured using the encryption and decryption are generated into the network in wireless sensor networks. The data are transferred through the nodes to be secured in the way of key generated to the base station using encryption and also the key generated in the destination for the purpose of decryption of the given data are secured way in the wireless sensor networks.

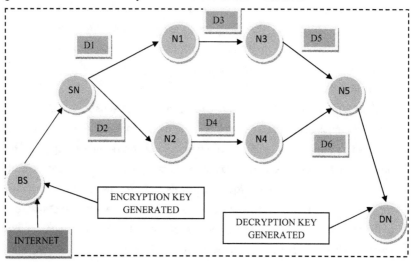

6.5 Block Cipher

The Energy Efficient provides the network security along with the small block size and key size using the block cipher [6]. We consider two block ciphers are the different energy performance in the wireless sensor networks. Characteristics of these ciphers are shown in Table I

Table 1: Characteristics of Block Ciphers

Block cipher	Block size	Key size
DES	64 bits	64 bits
AES	128 bits	128 bits

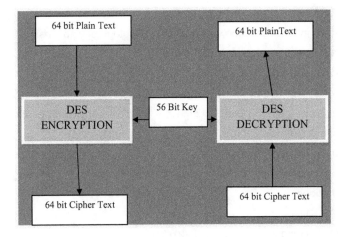

Figure 1: DES Block Diagram

6.6 Data Encryption Standard

DES is a symmetric key block cipher published by NIST. It takes 64 bit plain text and 64 bit cipher text both the encryption and decryption site [7]. The 56 bit cipher key is used for both encryption and decryption of the given data [8]. The encryption process is consists of two permutations (P-Boxes) are also called as initial and final permutations and also sixteen feistal rounds. Each Round with two elements consists of mixer and swapper. It is also called as invertible [9]. The decryption algorithm should be identical to the encryption algorithm in a reverse order. But in case of DES cipher, the encryption algorithm is so well designed, that the decryption algorithm is identical to the encryption algorithm only with the sub keys applied in the reverse order [10]. Feistel structure makes encryption and decryption processes.

6.7 DES Algorithm

1. Start the program
2. 64 input bits of clear text
3. 16 round keys are generated
4. Get the Initial Permutation and Final Permutation
5. Dividing into two 32 bits in the permutation.
6. Round Functions are generated left and right side of 64 bits of cipher text
7. Stop the program

6.8 RSA Algorithm

Diffie and Hellman introduced a new approach to cryptography to design a general-purpose encryption algorithm that satisfies the public-key encryption requirements. One of the first responses to the challenge was developed in 1977 by Ron Rivest, Adi Shamir, Len Adleman at MIT. Since then, the Rivest-Shamir-Adleman (RSA) scheme has become the most widely accepted and implemented general-purpose approach to public-key encryption [11].

Let's start with one of the simplest ciphers: General Caesar cipher. Its encryption and decryption operation can be represented using the following mathematical functions.

$$C = (P + K) \bmod 26 \ldots\ldots\ldots\ldots\ldots(1)$$
$$P = (C - K) \bmod 26 \ldots\ldots\ldots\ldots\ldots(2)$$

The RSA scheme is a block cipher. Each plaintext block is an integer between 0 and $n - 1$ for some n, which leads to a block size $\leq \log2 (n)$. The typical size for n is 1024 bits. The details of the RSA algorithm are described as follows.

6.9 RSA Algorithm

1) Get two large prime numbers p and q

2) Calculate $n = p \times q$;

3) Calculate $\_ (n) = (p - 1)(q - 1)$;

4) Pick e, so that gcd $(e, \_(n)) = 1, 1 < e < \_(n)$;

5) Calculate d, so that $d \cdot e \bmod \_ (n) = 1$, i.e., d is the multiplicative inverse of e in mod $\_ (n)$;

6) Get public key as KU = {e, n};

7) Get private key as KR = {d, n}.

6.10 Results and Discussion

This paper presents on Encryption and Decryption using DES algorithm and RSA algorithm is done by C ++Simulator. Results are shown in below. Figure 2: Shows the Node Results of the given Network. Figure 3: Shows that DES Encryption and Decryption and also Figure 4: Shows that RSA Encryption and Decryption. Figure 5: Shows that AES Encryption and Decryption. Figure 6: shows the energy consumption of the given network.

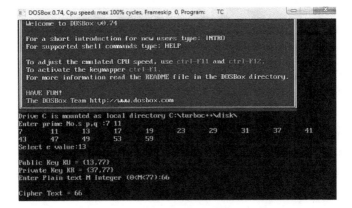

Figure 2: Node Results of the given Network

Figure 3: DES Encryption and Decryption.

Figure 4: RSA Encryption and Decryption

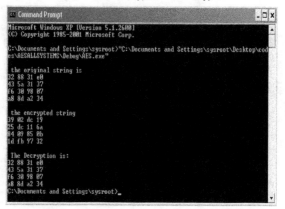

Figure 5: AES Encryption and Decryption

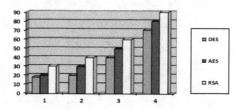

Figure 6: Energy Consumption

6.11 Conclusion

In this paper, we examine the energy efficiency of symmetric key cryptographic encryption algorithms applied in wireless sensor networks (WSNs) and in our study we consider block ciphers. Evaluating a number of symmetric key ciphers, we compare the energy performance of block ciphers applied to a WSN. Finally we conclude the data are transferred through the network are secured using the encryption and decryption in the way of energy efficiency to increases the life time of network in wireless sensor networks

.

References

[1]	Lingling Si,Zhigang Ji,Zhihui Wang," The Application of Symmetric Key Cryptographic Algorithms in Wireless Sensor Networks," Lingling Si et al. /Physics Procedia (2012)552 – 559

[2] Topology Control code, February 2010. Available from: <http:// code.google.com/p/protocon/>.

[3] OLSR-MC-NI, OLSR-TV code, and TopoView configuration, February 2010. Available from: <http://code.google.com/p/olsr/>.

[4] L. Dong, H. Liu, Y. Zhang, S. Paul, D.Raychaudhuri, On the Cache-and-Forward network architecture, in: Proceedings of the IEEE International Conference on Communications (ICC), 2009, pp. 1–5.

[5] H. Liu, Y. Zhang, D. Raychaudhuri, Performance evaluation of the Cache-and-Forward (CNF) network for mobile content delivery services, in: Proceedings of the IEEE International Conference on Communications (ICC), 2009, pp. 1–5.

[6] S. Paul, R. Yates, D. Raychaudhuri, Jim Kurose, The Cache-And- Forward network architecture for efficient mobile content delivery services in the future Internet, in: Proceedings of the First ITU-T Kaleidoscope Academic Conference on Innovations in NGN: Future Network and Services, 2008.

[7]	W. K. Koo, H. Lee, Y. H. Kim and D. H. Lee, "Implementation and Analysis of New Lightweight Cryptographic Algorithm Suitable for Wireless Sensor Networks," in Proc of 2008 Information Security and Assurance (ISA 2008), pp.73-76, Korea, April 2008.

[8]	M. Henricksen, "Tiny Dragon - An Encryption Algorithm for Wireless Sensor Networks," in Proc of 10th High Performance Computing and Communications, (HPCC '08), p.p. 795-800, 25-27 Sept. 2008.

[9] L. Bokor, L. Lois, C.A. Szabo, S. Szabo, Testbed of a novel media streaming architecture for heterogeneous wireless environment, in: Third International Conference on Testbeds and Research Infrastructure for the Development of Networks and Communities (TridentCom), May 2007.

[10] F. Jan, B. Mathieu, D. Meddour, Video streaming experiment on deployed ad hoc network, in: Third International Conference on Testbeds and Research Infrastructure for the Development of Networks and Communities TridentCom), May 2007.

[11] Y. Lin, A. Hamed Mohsenian Rad, V.W.S. Wong, J-H Song, Experimental comparisons between SAODV and AODV routing protocols, in: First ACM Workshop on Wireless Multimedia Networking and Performance Modeling, October 2005, pp. 113–122.

[12] E. Borgia, Experimental evaluation of ad hoc routing protocols, in: Third IEEE International Conference on Pervasive Computing and Communications Workshops, March 2005, pp. 232–236.

[13]   A. S. Wander, N. Gura, H. Eberle, V. Gupta, and S. C. Shantz, "Energy Analysis of Public-key Cryptography for Wireless Sensor Networks," in Proc of 2005 Pervasive Computing and Communications (PerCom 2005), pp. 324-328, Germany, March 2000

Chapter 7- Bandwidth Techniques in Wireless Sensor Networks

7.1 Overview

IEEE 802.11-based networks have been able to provide a certain level of quality of service (QoS) by the means of service differentiation, due to the IEEE 802.11e amendment. However, no mechanism or method has been standardized to accurately evaluate the amount of resources remaining on a given channel. Such an evaluation would, however, be a good asset for bandwidth-constrained applications. Consequently, despite the various contributions around this research topic, the estimation of the available bandwidth still represents one of the main issues in this field. In this, an improved mechanism to estimate the available bandwidth in IEEE 802.11-based ad hoc networks is proposed. Through simulations, the available bandwidths the quality of service parameters are computed.

7.2 Introduction

Adhoc networks are autonomous, self-organized, wireless, and mobile networks. They do not require setting up any fixed infrastructure such as access points, as the nodes organize themselves automatically to transfer data packets and manage topology changes due to mobility. Many of the current contributions in the ad hoc networking community assume that the underlying wireless technology is the IEEE 802.11 standard due to the broad availability of interface cards and simulation models. This standard provides an ad hoc mode, allowing mobiles to communicate directly. However, this standard has not been targeted especially for multihop ad-hoc operation, and it is therefore not perfectly suited to this type of networks.

Nowadays, several applications generate multimedia data flows or rely on the proper and efficient transmission of sensitive control traffic. These applications may benefit from a quality of service (QoS) support in the network. That is why this domain has been extensively studied and more and more QoS solutions are proposed for ad hoc networks. Some protocols intend to offer strong guarantees to the applications on the transmission characteristics, for instance bandwidth, delay, packet loss, or network load. Other solutions, which seem more suited to a mobile environment, only select the best route among all possible choices regarding the same criteria. In both cases, an accurate evaluation of the capabilities of the routes is necessary. The resource evaluation problem is far from being trivial as it must take into account several phenomena related to the wireless environment but also dependent on less measurable parameters such as the node mobility.

In this, a new method to evaluate the available bandwidth in ad hoc networks based on the IEEE 802.11 MAC layer is presented. This method uses the nodes' carrier sense capability combined to other techniques such as collision prediction to perform this estimation. It provides upper layers with an evaluation that represents an acceptable compromise between accuracy and measurement cost. Therefore, it is necessary to take into account the disruption that may be introduced in the network by the addition of a new flow and to distinguish between the raw throughput that may be transferred along a path and the maximum data rate that may be transferred without any noticeable interference. Hereafter, the available bandwidth between two neighbor nodes is defined as the maximum throughput that can be transmitted between these two peers without disrupting any already ongoing flow in the network. Link capacity is used to denote the maximum throughput a flow can achieve between two neighbor nodes regardless of other flows present in the network.

7.3 Bandwidth Estimation Techniques

Available bandwidth evaluation has generated several contributions in the wired and wireless networking communities. Several classifications of these solutions may be imagined. It is separated into the following two categories:

1. Estimation of the available bandwidth along a path is designated by active approaches the techniques that rely on the emission of dedicated end-to-end probe packets.

2. Other technique is designated by passive approaches the techniques that use only local information on the utilization of the bandwidth. A typical example of such approaches is a node monitoring the channel usage by sensing the radio medium. These mechanisms are usually transparent, but they may exchange information via one-hop broadcasts, as such information can be piggybacked in the Hello messages used by many routing protocols to discover the local topology.

7.4 Active Bandwidth Estimation Techniques

A detailed survey of the different techniques to evaluate the available bandwidth in wired networks is accessible in [1]. Measurements of the characteristics of this particular flow are performed at the receiver's side and then converted into an estimation of the end-to-end available bandwidth. Several protocols such as SLoPS [2] or TOPP [3] fall into this category. They mainly differ in the way they increase the packet sequence rate and in the metrics measured on the probing packet flow. It is worth noting that, with these techniques, the probing traffic may influence existing flows. Li et al. [4] propose to detect the presence of congestion by monitoring probe packets' delay. They propose a method to compute the medium utilization from such measurements and then derive the channel capacity from this channel usage ratio.

Based on the TOPP method, the authors of DietTOPP [5] evaluate the accuracy of such techniques in wireless networks. This work shows that both the probe packet size and the volume of cross-traffic have a stronger impact on the measured bandwidth in this environment than in wired networks. These techniques are, therefore, also very sensitive to the measurement parameters and easily lead to inaccurate results in a wireless environment. The active techniques cited above present, in addition, two major drawbacks regarding multihop ad hoc networks. First, when many nodes need to perform such an evaluation for several destinations, the amount of probe packets introduced in the network becomes important. It may, thus, interact with the data traffic and with other probes, modifying other estimations. Second, an end-to-end evaluation technique may not be as reactive as a local technique in a mobile context. When updating routes in response to node mobility or to a change in the available resources, local detection and reconstruction may be more efficient in several situations.

7.5 Passive Bandwidth Estimation Techniques

A dynamic bandwidth management scheme for single-hop ad hoc networks is proposed in [6]. In this solution, one node in the network hosts the Bandwidth Manager process, which is responsible for evaluating the available bandwidth in the cell and for allocating the bandwidth to each peer. Each node may ask the Bandwidth Manager for an exclusive access to the channel during a proportion of time using dedicated control messages. As the topology is reduced to a single cell, the available proportion time-share is computed by this entity considering that the total load is the sum of the individual loads. This approach can be considered as passive as very few control packets are exchanged, usually of small size. However, this solution is adapted to network topologies where all the nodes are within communication range but cannot be directly used in multihop ad hoc networks. Even if the election, the synchronization, and the maintenance of several Bandwidth Managers may represent a significant cost in large distributed networks, similar measurements may be employed. The method proposed in [7] uses such technique and adds a smoothing factor to hide transient effects. The QoS routing protocol designed in this paper is based on a simple estimation of the available bandwidth by each node and does not consider any interfering nodes. QoS-AODV [8] also performs such a per-node ABE. The evaluation mechanism constantly updates a value called Bandwidth Efficiency Ratio (BWER), which is the ratio between the numbers of transmitted and received packets.

The available bandwidth is simply obtained by multiplying the BWER value by the channel capacity. This ratio is broadcasted among the one-hop neighbors of each node through Hello messages. The bandwidth available to a node is then inferred from these values as the minimum of the available bandwidths over a closed single-hop neighborhood. QoS-AODV, therefore, considers not only the possibility to send a given amount of data but also the effect of the emissions of a node on its neighborhood.

In [9], Chaudet and Lassous proposed a bandwidth reservation protocol called Bandwidth Reservation under Interferences influence (BRuIT). This protocol's ABE mechanism takes into account the fact that, with the IEEE 802.11 standard, the carrier sense radius is larger than the transmission range. In other words, emitters share the bandwidth with other nodes they cannot communicate with. Experimental studies have shown that this carrier sense radius is at least twice the communication radius. To address this issue, each node regularly broadcasts to all its immediate neighbors information about the total bandwidth it uses to route and emit flows (deduced from applications and routing information) and its estimated available bandwidth. It also transmits similar information concerning all its one-hop neighbors, propagating such information at a two-hop distance. Each node then performs admission control based on this two-hop neighborhood knowledge. When the carrier sense radius is equal to twice the communication radius, the authors have shown that two-hop communication represents the best compromise between estimation accuracy and cost [10].Making the same observation, Yaling and Kravets [11] proposed the Contention Aware Admission Control Protocol (CACP). In this framework, each node first computes its local proportion of idle channel time by monitoring the radio medium. Then, the authors propose three different techniques to propagate this information to the greatest number of nodes within the carrier sense area. First, similarly to BRuIT, they propose to include the information in Hello messages to reach the two-hop neighborhood. Second, they propose to increase the nodes' transmission power; however, this emission power is often limited by regulations and this technique may therefore only be applicable when power control is used for regular transmissions. Finally, receiving nodes can also reduce their sensitivity in order to decode information coming from farther away, which depends on the quality of electronics and on the signal modulation. Similarly to [12], the authors also point out the existence of intraflow contention. When a flow takes a multihop route, successive routers contend for channel access for frames belonging to the same flow. It is thus important to take into account at least the route length when performing admission control. Ideally, the exact interactions between nodes along a path should be identified and considered. Finally, the AAC protocol, proposed in [13], makes each node consider the set of potential contenders as a single node. It measures the activity period durations and considers that any such period can be seen as a frame emission of the corresponding length. With this mechanism, collisions and distant emissions are also considered when computing the medium occupancy. Based on this measurement, each node is able to evaluate its available bandwidth.

7.6 Proposed System

It is quite tricky, from an operational point of view, to evaluate the performance of the sole ABE part of an existing QoS protocol. Therefore, for comparison purposes, the previously described bandwidth evaluation technique ABE is integrated into a protocol and implemented it under NS-2. This simulator has been chosen because of the availability of other protocol models. ABE is chosen to integrate into AODV, in order to be similar to BRuIT, QoS-AODV, or AAC. The impact of the estimation technique on the bandwidth management in the network is studied by comparing the performance of the different protocols. The protocol is called hereafter ABE-AODV.

7.7 ABE Features

In ABE-AODV, neighboring nodes exchange their available bandwidth computed locally via Hello messages. Every Δ seconds, each node locally estimates its medium occupancy ratio and includes this information in a Hello packet. These values are then converted into link evaluations using the final available bandwidth (1).

The accuracy of the bandwidth evaluation obviously depends on the value of Δ, which can be considered as a sampling period. The larger Δ is, the more stable the measurements will be, hiding fast variations in the medium load. However Δ, should also be small enough to allow fast reactions to long-term load variations and to node mobility.

Hello-based techniques generate additional overhead depending on the Hello emission frequency. Ideally, the Hello packet emission frequency should be adapted to the node mobility and/or to the flow dynamics. In order to have meaningful comparisons, we chose to fix this value to $\Delta = 1$ second in ABE-AODV. Similarly, all compared protocols are tuned accordingly to emit one information frame each second.

We have slightly modified AODV in order to transform it into a QoS protocol based on ABE. It thus becomes a cross-layer routing protocol. The MAC layer estimates proactively and periodically the available bandwidth of the neighboring links, and the routing layer is in charge of discovering QoS routes complying to the application demands, basing its decisions on the MAC layer information.

7.8 Route Discovery

The aim of the route discovery procedure is to find a route between the sender and the receiver that meets the constraints specified by the application level in terms of bandwidth. Therefore, two flows with the same source and destination can follow different routes depending on the network state.

Each mobile node that receives such an RREQ performs an admission control by simply comparing the bandwidth requirement carried in the RREQ packet to the estimated available bandwidth on the link it received the RREQ on. If this check is positive, the node adds its own address to the route and forwards the RREQ; otherwise, it silently discards the message. This step is different from the other tested protocols as the admission control is done at the receiver side and not at the sender side. This is explained by the fact that, in

ABE, each node stores the available bandwidths of its ingoing links. Finally, if the destination receives a first RREQ, it sends a unicast route reply (RREP) to the initiator of the request along the reverse path.

7.9 Intra Flow Contractions Problem

Simply comparing the bandwidth application requirement and a link available bandwidth is not sufficient to decide about the network ability to convey a flow. Indeed, the intraflow contention problem has to be considered when performing multihop admission control.

In [12], the authors compute a value called contention count (CC) of a node along a given path. This value is equal to the number of nodes on the multihop path that are located within the carrier sensing range of the considered node. To calculate the CC of each node, the authors analyze the distribution of the signal power.

As in [17], for simplicity reasons, in ABE, we rather use a direct relationship between the end-to-end throughput and the number of hops. Hence, after consideration of the intraflow contention on an intermediate node j, which is located at H hops from the source and has received the RREQ from a node i, the available bandwidth considered for admission control, denoted by B (i,j), is equal to

$$B(i,j) = \frac{Efinal(b(i,j))}{min\ (H, 4)}$$

Where $E_{final}(b_{(i,j)})$ is the available bandwidth of link (i,j) as computed by ABE

7.10 Results and Discussion

Table 1 General Parameters for Simulations

Parameters	Values
HELLO interval	1 sec
Packets size	1000 bytes
Medium capacity	2 Mb/s or 11Mb/s
Communication range (2 Mb/s)	250 m
Carrier sensing range (2 Mb/s)	550 m
Communication range (11 Mb/s)	160 m

Carrier sensing range (11 Mb/s)	350 m
Grid Size	1000 m * 1000 m
C (Number of retransmissions)	6

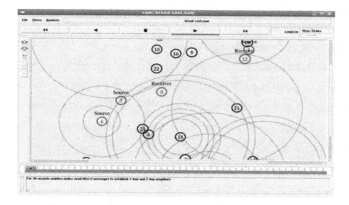

Figure 1 Describing the Process

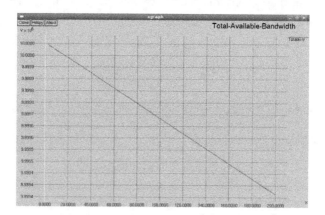

Figure 2 X-Graphs for the Total Available Bandwidth

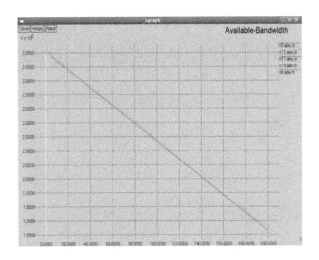

Figure 3 X-Graphs for the Available Bandwidth

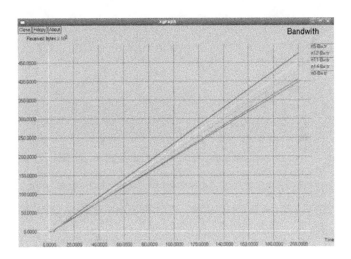

Figure 4 X- Graphs for the Bandwidth Of Various Nodes

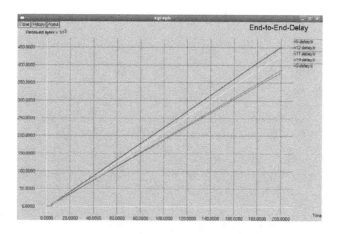

Figure 5 X-graphs for the end-to-end delay of various nodes

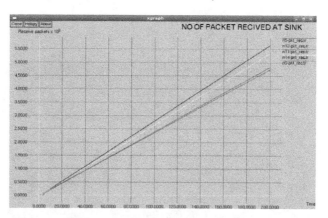

Figure 6 X-graphs for no. Of packets received at sink of various nodes

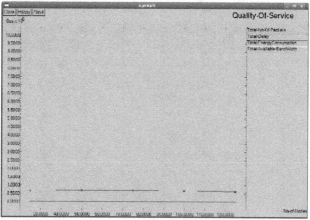

Figure 7 (A) X-Graphs for the Various Parameters OF QOS for Different No. Of Nodes

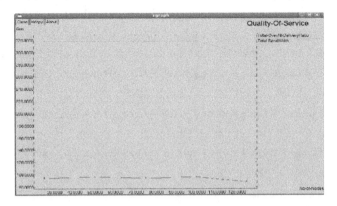

Figure 7(b) X-Graphs for the Various Parameters OF QOS for different No. Of Nodes

7.11 Conclusion

A new technique to compute the available bandwidth between two neighbor nodes and by extension along a path is presented. This method combines channel monitoring to estimate each node's medium occupancy including distant emissions, probabilistic combination of these values to account for synchronization between nodes, estimation of the collision probability between each couple of nodes, and variable overhead's impact estimation. Results are encouraging in fixed networks as well as in mobile networks. These scenarios prove that the most difficult point when designing a QoS protocol is not the routing process but the estimation of available resources through the network. As future works, two issues can be focused. First, in this current evaluation, no difference between the bandwidth consumed by QoS flows and the bandwidth consumed by best effort flows is made. Therefore, it may be possible that a node considers its available bandwidth on a link as almost null whereas the whole bandwidth is consumed by best effort flows. Decreasing the rate of these flows may lead to a higher acceptance rate of QoS flows. Differentiating flow types may also result in a better utilization of the network resources. In parallel, the delay metric can be investigated

References

[1] R. Prasad, M. Murray, C. Dovrolis, and K. Claffy, "Bandwidth Estimation: Metrics, Measurement Techniques, and Tools," IEEE Network, vol. 17, no. 6, pp. 27-35, Nov. 2003.

[2] M. Jain and C. Dovrolis, "End-to-End Available Bandwidth: Measurement Methodology, Dynamics, and Relation with TCP Throughput," IEEE/ACM Trans. Networking (TON '03), vol. 11,no. 4, pp. 537-549, Aug. 2003.

[3] B. Melander, M. Bjorkman, and P. Gunningberg, "A New Endto- End Probing Analysis Method for Estimating Bandwidth Bottlenecks," Proc. Fifth Global Internet Symp. (Global Internet) held in conjunction with Global Comm. Conf. (GLOBECOM '00), Nov. 2000.

[4] F.Y. Li, M. Haugea, A. Hafslund, O. Kure, and P. Spilling, "Estimating Residual Bandwidth in 802.11-Based Ad Hoc Networks: An Empirical Approach," Proc. Seventh Int'l Symp. Wireless Personal Multimedia Comm. (WPMC '04), Sept. 2004.

[5] A. Johnsson, B. Melander, and M. Bjo¨rkman, "Bandwidth Measurement in Wireless Network," technical report, Ma¨lardalen Univ., Mar. 2005.

[6] S.H. Shah, K. Chen, and K. Nahrstedt, "Dynamic Bandwidth Management for Single-Hop Ad Hoc Wireless Networks," Proc. First IEEE Int'l Conf. Pervasive Computing and Comm. (PerCom '03), Aug. 2003.

[7] K. Xu, K. Tang, R. Bagrodia, M. Gerla, and M. Bereschinsky, "Adaptive Bandwidth Management and QoS Provisioning in Large Scale Ad Hoc Networks," Proc. Military Comm. Conf. (MILCOM '03), Oct. 2003.

[8] R. de Renesse, M. Ghassemian, V. Friderikos, and A.H. Aghvami, "QoS Enabled Routing in Mobile Ad Hoc Networks," Proc. IEE Fifth Int'l Conf. 3G Mobile Comm. Technologies (IEE 3G), 2004.

[9] C. Chaudet and I.G. Lassous, "BRuIT—Bandwidth Reservation under InTerferences Influence," Proc. European Wireless (EW '02), Feb. 2002.

[10] C. Chaudet and I.G. Lassous, "Evaluation of the BRuIT Protocol," Proc. IEEE 61st Semiann. Vehicular Technology Conf. (VTC Spring '05), May 2005.

[11] Y. Yang and R. Kravets, "Contention Aware Admission Control for Ad Hoc Networks," IEEE Trans. Mobile Computing, vol. 4,pp. 363-377, 2005.

[12] K. Sanzgiri, I.D. Chakeres, and E.M. Belding-Royer, "Determining Intra-Flow Contention along Multihop Paths in Wireless Networks," Proc. First Int'l Conf. Broadband Networks (BROADNETS '04), Oct. 2004.

[13] R. de Renesse, M. Ghassemian, V. Friderikos, and A.H. Aghvami, "Adaptive Admission Control for Ad Hoc and Sensor Networks Providing Quality of Service," technical report, King College London, May 2005.

[14] V. Bharghavan, A.J. Demers, S. Shenker, and L. Zhang, "MACAW: A Media Access Protocol for Wireless LAN's," Proc. ACM SIGCOMM '94, pp. 212-225, 1994.

[15] C. Sarr, C. Chaudet, G. Chelius, and I.G. Lassous, "A Node-Based Available Bandwidth Evaluation in IEEE 802.11 Ad Hoc Networks," Int'l J. Parallel, Emergent and Distributed Systems, vol. 21, no. 6, 2006.

[16] G. Bianchi, "Performance Analysis of the IEEE 802.11 Distributed Coordination Function," J. Selected Areas in Comm., vol. 18, no. 3, pp. 535-547, Mar. 2000.

[17] L. Chen and W. Heinzelman, "QoS-Aware Routing Based on Bandwidth Estimation for Mobile Ad Hoc Networks," IEEE J. Selected Areas of Comm., vol. 3, 2005.

Publisher: Eliva Press SRL

Email: info@elivapress.com

Eliva Press is an independent publishing house established for the publication and dissemination of academic works all over the world. Company provides high quality and professional service for all of our authors.

Our Services:
Free of charge, open-minded, eco-friendly, innovational.

-All services are free of charge for you as our author (manuscript review, step-by-step book preparation, publication, distribution, and marketing).
-No financial risk. The author is not obliged to pay any hidden fees for publication.
-Editors. Dedicated editors will assist step by step through the projects.
-Money paid to the author for every book sold. Up to 50% royalties guaranteed.
-ISBN (International Standard Book Number). We assign a unique ISBN to every Eliva Press book.
-Digital archive storage. Books will be available online for a long time. We don't need to have a stock of our titles. No unsold copies. Eliva Press uses environment friendly print on demand technology that limits the needs of publishing business. We care about environment and share these principles with our customers.
-Cover design. Cover art is designed by a professional designer.
-Worldwide distribution. We continue expanding our distribution channels to make sure that all readers have access to our books.

www.elivapress.com

www.ingramcontent.com/pod-product-compliance
Lightning Source LLC
LaVergne TN
LVHW052312060326
832902LV00021B/3838